Original title:
Unraveling the Unknown

Copyright © 2024 Creative Arts Management OÜ
All rights reserved.

Author: Robert Ashford
ISBN HARDBACK: 978-9916-90-290-5
ISBN PAPERBACK: 978-9916-90-291-2

The Labyrinthine Search for Meaning

In shadows deep, I wander lost,
Paths entwined, I count the cost.
Each turn reveals a choice anew,
Threads of fate, both old and true.

Mirrors reflect what I refuse,
In every glance, the silent clues.
Questions linger, never fade,
In the silence, truths are laid.

Footfalls echo in the mist,
Memories swirl, too sweet to resist.
Yet what I seek, I cannot find,
Elusive thoughts, a tangled mind.

Through twists and turns, my heart does race,
Yearning for that familiar place.
In the dark, I seek the light,
A compass guiding through the night.

Whispers from the Edge of Forever

In twilight's glow, the voices hum,
Soft secrets speak, a distant drum.
They weave through trees, around the bend,
Echoes of a world that will not end.

Stars above in silent dance,
Invite the heart to take a chance.
With every breath, the cosmos sighs,
In whispers, hope beneath the skies.

The horizon bleeds in vibrant hues,
Tales of old, and dreams to choose.
With every heartbeat, ancient lore,
Calls me closer to the shore.

As time unfolds its tender hand,
Moments drift like grains of sand.
I listen deep, the night will tell,
Of secrets held, where shadows dwell.

Threads of Forgotten Dreams

In a tapestry of night,
Whispers drift like dust,
Colors fade from sight,
Once vibrant, now a rust.

Echoes linger softly,
Memories softly weave,
In the heart's lost coffee,
Hope we still believe.

Each dream a fragile thread,
Pulled gently from the past,
In slumber's quiet bed,
Each moment meant to last.

Yet dawn will break the spell,
And daylight steals away,
What once was ours to tell,
Now melds with yesterday.

Woven into Silence

Threads of silence twine,
Stitched in shadows deep,
Words unspoken shine,
In the secrets we keep.

The fabric softly hums,
Beneath a moonlit glow,
Echoes of what comes,
Are lost in the flow.

Woven tight with care,
Patterns of the heart,
Each pull, a hidden layer,
In the quiet art.

In the stillness, hear,
The stories that reside,
In whispers sincere,
Where the secrets abide.

Harvesting Secrets of the Soul

In fields of whispered thought,
We gather what was lost,
The treasures that we sought,
At an unmeasured cost.

Each secret like a seed,
Planted deep in the night,
In shadows we shall feed,
On the dreams that take flight.

With hands both warm and open,
We toil the fertile ground,
In silence, words unspoken,
Yield the truths we have found.

Harvests rich with grace,
Laden with gentle fruit,
In every quiet space,
The soul's wisdom takes root.

The Allure of Shadows

In twilight's gentle grip,
Shadows dance and sway,
A soft and silent slip,
Into the end of day.

Mysteries entwine,
In corners, dim and cold,
Where thoughts intertwine,
And stories go untold.

The allure of the night,
Calls softly to the brave,
In darkness, there's a light,
In the depths we must save.

Beneath the starry veil,
Whispers start to bloom,
In silence, we set sail,
Finding solace in gloom.

The Language of Stars

Whispers of ancient light,
Flicker in the dark of night.
Each twinkle tells a tale,
In cosmic winds, dreams set sail.

Galaxies spin and dance,
In a timeless, vast expanse.
Constellations draw their lines,
Mapping fate with silent signs.

The heart listens, eyes wide,
To the secrets stars confide.
Messages from far-off spheres,
Hopes entwined in cosmic years.

In the stillness, we find grace,
In the spaces, a warm embrace.
For in the void, love is found,
The universe sings, a gentle sound.

Beneath the Surface

Ripples whisper on the lake,
Mysteries of the world awake.
Layers deep, stories hide,
Beneath the surface, truth resides.

Silent currents, shadows creep,
Where the secrets of the deep.
Echoes of a gentle tide,
In the depths, dreams coincide.

Fish dart like thoughts in flight,
In watery realms, pure delight.
A dance beneath the azure sky,
Where the stillness softly lies.

Boundless realms of thoughts untold,
In the depth, wonders unfold.
Nature's voice, serene and pure,
Beneath the surface, hearts endure.

Chasing Shadows

Fleeting forms in twilight's grace,
Dance along a moonlit place.
Softly shifting, swift as breath,
Chasing shadows, flirts with death.

Through the whispers of the trees,
Echoes float upon the breeze.
In the dusk, dreams rise and fall,
As shadows stretch and softly call.

Footsteps sound on gravel paths,
Filled with yearning, love's warm laughs.
In the chase, we seek to find,
The essence of the heart and mind.

Elusive, they weave and sway,
Guiding hearts that wish to play.
In the twilight's gentle fold,
Chasing shadows, stories told.

The Silence of Secrets

In quiet corners, whispers dwell,
Tales locked away, hard to tell.
Silence wraps its gentle arms,
Holding close forgotten charms.

Beneath the surface, veils are drawn,
In shadows where the night has grown.
Echoed truths in muted sighs,
In hush, the heart of secrets lies.

The weight of words left unsaid,
Lingering long, filling with dread.
Yet in the stillness, hope can bloom,
As light dispels the heavy gloom.

So let the silence softly break,
A fragile bond, a careful ache.
For in the truth, we find release,
In the silence, lies our peace.

Veiled Horizons of Thought

In shadows deep where whispers dwell,
Ideas flicker, like a secret spell.
A canvas vast, the mind's own art,
Each stroke a journey, a thought to impart.

Horizons blur, yet clarity is near,
With every step, the vision clears.
Through veils of doubt, in silence sought,
We chase the echoes of the mind's own thought.

Above the clouds, the sky unfolds,
A tapestry where the future holds.
In twilight dreams, our spirits rise,
To dance with constellations in the skies.

So let us wander on paths unseen,
In the realm of thought, where we glean.
With open hearts and fearless quest,
We'll find the truths, the very best.

The Language of Hidden Realms

In whispers soft the ancients speak,
In riddles curled and shadows sleek.
Their stories weave a tapestry fine,
Of worlds beyond, where stars align.

Each note a bridge, each sigh a clue,
To realms where dreams thread the dew.
Through silent glades and crystal streams,
The language flows like moonlit beams.

Here secrets swirl in cosmic dance,
Inviting souls to take a chance.
With hearts attuned to mysteries deep,
In hidden realms, our spirits leap.

So let us listen, learn, and roam,
In this vast universe, we find our home.
For every word holds magic's grace,
In the language of the hidden space.

Dreams Lost in the Maze

In corridors of thought, I roam,
Lost in dreams that feel like home.
Each twist and turn, a fleeting glimpse,
Of shadows dancing, a thought that limps.

The walls close in, a daunting sight,
Yet within the dark, there sparks the light.
With every breath, I seek the true,
In the heart of the maze, I'll find my view.

Echoes call from pathways long,
A melody both haunting and strong.
Through tangled roads, I'll seek the prize,
A hidden truth beyond the lies.

So onward through this labyrinth vast,
With hope as guide, I'll hold steadfast.
For every dream, though sometimes lost,
Is worth the journey, no matter the cost.

The Geometry of Infinite Possibilities

In lines and angles, the world unfolds,
A dance of shapes with stories told.
Each point a spark, each curve a chance,
In the geometry of life's great dance.

Figures rise, a structure new,
Forming paths where ideas brew.
With every turn, horizons shift,
In this realm, our spirits lift.

Infinity known in circles drawn,
In sacred spaces, from dusk to dawn.
Every vertex a moment's grace,
The world alive in endless embrace.

So let us sketch these dreams anew,
With bold strokes of vibrant hue.
For in this art, our souls will find,
The beauty held in a curious mind.

Hidden in Plain Sight

In shadows where secrets breathe,
Whispers curl like autumn leaves.
Eyes may search but seldom find,
Beauty hides, yet stays entwined.

A fleeting glance, a subtle sound,
Moments pass, yet truth abounds.
Hidden gems in daily strife,
Lurking close, this vivid life.

In crowded streets or quiet nooks,
Stories linger in the books.
Unseen ties that softly bind,
Hearts and thoughts, so intertwined.

Look again with patient grace,
In stillness, find a warm embrace.
For what you seek is often near,
Hidden truths will soon appear.

Beyond the Horizon

The sun dips low, the stars ignite,
Dreams emerge in the velvet night.
Waves of hope on distant shores,
Unfolding tales, forever soars.

Mountains stand with stoic pride,
Whispers of winds that softly guide.
In the distance, visions gleam,
Yonder lies a waking dream.

With every step, new paths will wind,
To realms where limits are unlined.
Chasing echoes on the breeze,
Beyond the horizon, hearts find ease.

Adventure calls with each sunrise,
Opening doors to endless skies.
In every journey, truth recites,
The beauty found beyond the sights.

Dimensional Horizons

Layers thick, where time does bend,
Parallel paths, each twist an end.
In this realm of unseen sights,
Dimensions dance in starry nights.

Echoes bounce from worlds unknown,
Whispers swirl, yet stand alone.
In this tapestry we weave,
Infinite threads are hard to perceive.

Time a river, flowing wide,
Moments collide, and worlds collide.
Every heartbeat, a chance to see,
The myriad forms of you and me.

Venture forth, let spirits fly,
In the realm where dreams comply.
Beyond horizons yet untold,
Infinite wonders wait to unfold.

The Art of Questioning

Inquiring minds seek and roam,
Each question crafts a path to home.
The heart of knowledge beats within,
Curiosity begins to spin.

What lies behind the hidden door?
What treasures wait on distant shore?
Every query a spark of light,
Illuminates the world in sight.

Folded truths and twisted clues,
Wisdom flows from the answers you choose.
With each "why" and "how" we find,
Layers unveil, expanding mind.

Embrace the journey, never cease,
For in each question, there's release.
The art of wondering, sweet and bright,
Opens worlds from darkness to light.

Threads of the Unseen

In the quiet dark, whispers weave,
Tales untold, the heart believes.
Invisible strings, softly bind,
Echoes of love, time left behind.

Through dreams we wander, yet unseen,
Moments captured, pure and clean.
Laughter lingers, shadows play,
Threads unite, and drift away.

Beneath the stars, they intertwine,
Secrets shared, a sacred sign.
Promises linger, not in view,
Binding us close, me and you.

In every heartbeat, warmth remains,
Silent stories, joy and pains.
Threads of fate, forever spun,
Linking souls, two become one.

Veils of Mystery

Fog rolls in, a soft embrace,
Hiding secrets, time and space.
Each step taken, hushed and light,
Veils of mystery, cloaked in night.

Whispers follow, shadows dance,
Life's riddles call, a tempting chance.
Questions rise as stars are born,
Hidden truths, softly worn.

Through the mist, a flicker shines,
Years of waiting, tangled lines.
Around each corner, wonder waits,
Veils of dreams, elusive fates.

In silence lies the heart's refrain,
Every answer hides the pain.
But beneath the shroud, love glows,
Warmed by secrets only known.

Threads of the Unseen

Drawn together, souls connect,
In the void, a deep respect.
Weaving paths through joy and strife,
Threads unseen, the fabric of life.

In every glance, a spark ignites,
Shared memories, countless nights.
Unwritten stories, soft and true,
Tales of me, entwined with you.

Winding roads that fade away,
Moments cherished, come what may.
Invisible threads begin to show,
Linking pasts that overflow.

As the sun sets, shadows merge,
Hearts in rhythm, thoughts converge.
With gentle hands, we shape our fate,
Threads of love, never too late.

Secrets Beneath the Surface

Beneath the calm, the ripples hide,
Mysteries swim, time and tide.
Glimmers of truth, briefly revealed,
Secrets whispered, hearts concealed.

Waves that dance with soft caress,
Tales of longing, oft to guess.
In the depths, tales interlace,
Hidden dreams in a sacred space.

Echoes murmur from the deep,
Guarding wishes, thoughts we keep.
With every plunge, we find our way,
Secrets unveiled, come what may.

In twilight's glow, reflections fade,
Memories linger, never betrayed.
For below the surface, lies the key,
Unlocking paths to you and me.

Forgotten Corners

Dusty shelves and shadows play,
Whispers of the past decay.
In silent rooms where echoes call,
Lost moments linger, shadows fall.

Maps of time with faded ink,
In every crack, the memories sink.
Cornerstones of what once stood still,
Fragments of life, a ghostly thrill.

The air is thick with stories old,
Of hearts once brave, now muted, cold.
In forgotten corners, we ignite,
A spark of hope, a faint light bright.

Let us wander where few have tread,
Through wild paths where old dreams bled.
In every hushed and hidden space,
Lives a memory we must embrace.

Tangled Realities

Threads of fate in woven dreams,
Twisted paths with vibrant themes.
Reality bends in soft embrace,
In each corner, a hidden face.

Time entwines in spiraled leaps,
Secrets buried, silence keeps.
In every choice a ripple flows,
The fabric changes, nobody knows.

Mirrored visions, reflections blur,
In tangled webs, we're unsure.
Lost in mazes, we seek the key,
To unravel what's meant to be.

As night falls, the stars align,
Infinite paths, a fate divine.
In tangled realities, we may find,
A truth that dances, undefined.

Fragments of Truth

Scattered pieces on the floor,
Jigsaw puzzles we explore.
In shadows deep, a glimmer bright,
Fragments whisper in the night.

Each shard holds a tale, a spark,
In every silence, echoes hark.
The puzzle waits for hands to mold,
Stories arise, both brave and bold.

In conversations lost in time,
We chase the rhyme, the perfect line.
Through cracks of doubt, our hearts pursue,
The bitter-sweet of fragments true.

To find the whole within the piece,
In varied truths, we seek release.
Amidst the chaos, beauty lies,
In fragments of truth, our spirit flies.

Enigma of the Infinite

Stars that twinkle, secrets hold,
In the vastness, stories told.
Eternal dance of dark and light,
In wonders deep, we take flight.

Whispers of the galaxy call,
In cosmic fields, we rise and fall.
Time a river, never still,
In the infinite, hearts to fill.

Questions linger, answers flee,
In every question, a mystery.
The enigma wrapped in dreams we weave,
In moments shared, we dare believe.

Across the cosmos, we shall roam,
In the enigma, we find home.
Infinite paths, stories entwine,
In each heartbeat, a spark divine.

In Search of Silent Truths

Amidst the noise of fleeting days,
We seek the whispers of lost ways.
In shadows deep, the answers dwell,
In silent truths, our souls can tell.

The rush of life obscures the light,
Yet in the dark, we find what's right.
A gentle nudge, a fleeting thought,
In quiet moments, all is sought.

The heart knows paths that logic shuns,
In stillness, clarity becomes.
With every step, we start to see,
The silent truths that set us free.

To listen close, to pause, to breathe,
In every heartbeat, we believe.
A journey ventured, not in haste,
In search of truths, our fears laid waste.

The Hidden Corners of the Heart

In corners dim where shadows creep,
Lies secrets that our wishes keep.
A tender sigh, a whispered word,
In hidden spaces, love's oft heard.

Among the thorns, a rose will bloom,
In quiet moments, banish gloom.
Each heartbeat echoes tales untold,
In hidden corners, warmth unfolds.

Cloaked in silence, emotions soar,
With every glance, we yearn for more.
In laughter shared, or tears that flow,
The heart's hidden corners gently glow.

To seek the truth in lost embrace,
In every doubt, a tender grace.
With every beat, we find our way,
In hidden corners, hearts will stay.

Mysteries Wrapped in Time's Embrace

In layers deep, the past concealed,
In fleeting moments, truths revealed.
Whispers echo through ages lost,
In time's embrace, we bear the cost.

Each tick of clock, a story spins,
In shadows cast, where journeys begin.
With every step, we touch the line,
Of mysteries that forever twine.

In twilight's glow, the secrets breathe,
Of dreams and hopes that interweave.
To chase the past is to abide,
In mysteries where time resides.

So let us dance through veils of years,
With open hearts and joyful tears.
In time's embrace, we find our place,
Wrapped in the warmth of love's embrace.

The Allure of the Darkened Path

Beneath the stars, where shadows play,
An unseen road awaits our stay.
With each step forward, doubts arise,
Yet in the dark, true courage lies.

Through tangled woods, the whispers call,
In silence deep, we feel it all.
A flicker light, a guiding spark,
The allure grows within the dark.

With every turn, new dreams ignite,
In somber hues, there's hidden light.
To walk the path that few have seen,
Is to embrace what might have been.

So take my hand, let's venture near,
In darkened paths, we conquer fear.
For in the night, our spirits soar,
To find the wonder, forevermore.

The Silent Pulse of Questions

In the dark, a whisper flows,
Questions linger, silence grows.
Softly tugging at the heart,
Each inquiry, a work of art.

Moments captured, yet unmade,
Shadows dance in twilight's shade.
Answers hide beneath the skin,
Open doors that draw us in.

Time remains a restless muse,
Chasing dreams we seldom choose.
In the quiet, truths unfold,
Secrets waiting to be told.

Through the stillness, voices rise,
Yearning for the wisest skies.
With each pulse, we seek the light,
Finding meaning in the night.

Mysterious Footprints in the Sand

Along the shore, the tides retreat,
Footprints vanish in the heat.
Whispers carried by the breeze,
Echoes of forgotten seas.

Curved and twisted, lines so shy,
Tales they tell of days gone by.
Who walked here, where did they roam?
In the grains, we sense a home.

Waves will wash the traces clear,
Yet the memories feel so near.
Every step a fleeting chance,
A dance that time could not enhance.

Footprints fade, but dreams remain,
Imprints held within the grain.
Each new tide, a cycle spun,
In the sand, our stories run.

Portraits of the Unseen

In shadows deep, the figures blend,
Silent gazes that won't bend.
Faces formed by fleeting light,
Fractured glimpses of the night.

Canvas stretched on empty walls,
Whispers echo through the halls.
Every glance a tale untold,
Mysteries that dare unfold.

Color fades in muted tones,
Yet the essence still intones.
With each stroke, a life ignites,
Flashes of forgotten nights.

Unseen portraits draw us near,
In their gaze, a haunting sphere.
Captured souls in silent dreams,
In the quiet, nothing seems.

Haunting Echoes in Stillness

In the chill of night's embrace,
Echos linger, weightless grace.
Whispers brush the edges fine,
Time suspends at the borderline.

Every sound a phantom note,
Memories that gently float.
In the void, a quiet hum,
Soft as shadows yet to come.

Stillness thick with tales to share,
Voices lost upon the air.
Listen closely, hearts may hear,
Echoed truths we hold so dear.

Haunting notes in twilight's glow,
Guide us where the spirits flow.
In the silence, we discern,
Lessons from the echoes learn.

Patterns of the Unperceived

Silent whispers drift through time,
Echoes of dreams not yet defined.
Colors dance in shadowed light,
Unseen wonders come to sight.

In the corners of our minds,
Mysteries weaving, intertwined.
Simple joys and hidden fears,
Call to us through all the years.

Threads of fate, so finely spun,
Interlace until we're one.
In each moment, subtle grace,
Patterns form, we find our place.

Life unfolds in quiet ways,
Secrets kept for future days.
In the stillness, we may find,
The beauty of the unperceived kind.

Navigating the Veiled Maze

Through the corridors of thought,
Labyrinth paths, lessons sought.
Twists and turns, a haunting round,
In the silence, truth is found.

Shadows linger, doubts arise,
Veils conceal the hidden skies.
Every corner holds a clue,
Guiding hearts to something new.

Footsteps echo, softly laid,
Memories in twilight fade.
With each turn, we learn and yearn,
For the light, our souls to burn.

Navigating in the night,
Searching for the distant light.
Though the maze may feel so vast,
Hope remains, our guiding cast.

The Dimensions of What Lurks

In the stillness, something stirs,
Echoes swirl like whispered purrs.
What we sense, yet cannot see,
Lurking just beyond the tree.

Shapes that shift with shadow's grace,
Crafting secrets in their space.
Tales of old and fears unvoiced,
In the silence, we're rejoiced.

Every heartbeat draws us near,
The unknown, both bright and drear.
Dimensions fold and intertwine,
What lurks whispers, "You are mine."

In the dark, the truth unveils,
Woven deep in hidden trails.
What persists, both strange and bright,
Calls to us, igniting light.

Beyond the Horizon of Knowledge

Waves of thought crash on the shore,
What lies beyond, we can't ignore.
Fathoms deep, the questions rise,
Venturing past familiar skies.

Each horizon holds its dreams,
Buried in the flowing streams.
Maps of mind, not yet explored,
Boundless realms we can't afford.

Stepping forth with hearts ablaze,
Curiosity obeys.
Limitless, the stars we chase,
In the unknown, we find our grace.

Beyond what we can fully know,
Seeds of wisdom start to grow.
In every breath, in every choice,
Beyond the horizon, we rejoice.

When Questions Take Flight

Whispers rise into the air,
Curiosity begins to share.
From the ground, we seek the sky,
With every question, spirits fly.

Doubt and wonder intertwine,
In the heart, where dreams align.
Each inquiry a spark of light,
Illuminating the quiet night.

Wings of thought on breezes soar,
A journey painted evermore.
We embrace the unknown's call,
With courage, we will never fall.

Journey Through the Uncharted

Steps taken on a path anew,
With horizons flashing blue.
Every twist hides tales untold,
In the wild, our hearts grow bold.

Mountains rise and rivers flow,
In the midst of breezes blow.
We wander past the fading night,
Our hopes, a constant guiding light.

Each moment sparks the thrill of now,
On this journey, we will vow.
To seek beyond the stars so bright,
In the dark, we find our sight.

The Labyrinth of Secrets

Twists and turns in shadows deep,
Guarded truths the silence keeps.
In the maze, we dare to tread,
With each step, new fears are fed.

Whispers echo, paths divide,
In the night, we must confide.
Keith the way with hearts aglow,
Through the dark, we seek to know.

Hidden doors and silent keys,
Open spaces, gentle breezes.
In the depths of night, we find,
The secrets echo in our mind.

Shrouded in Ambiguity

Fog rolls in, the world is blurred,
Every thought feels quite unheard.
In this haze, we drift and sway,
Lost in dreams that fade away.

Colors blend, and lines grow thin,
What is truth, and where begins?
In the twilight, shadows play,
As we dance through shades of gray.

Questions linger, answers hide,
Within the stillness, fears abide.
Yet in the murk, hope still gleams,
Lighting up our quiet dreams.

The Unfolding of Riddles

In shadows cast by whispered tales,
Secrets dance in moonlit veils.
Questions echo without a sound,
In the labyrinth, lost and found.

Chasing answers beyond the door,
Every step reveals much more.
Threads of fate weave tight and neat,
Puzzle pieces at our feet.

The heart of truth, a fragile thread,
Mystery sleeps in words unsaid.
With every twist, the riddle spins,
In quiet moments, wisdom begins.

So seek the light through darkened trees,
Where silence hums a gentle breeze.
Awake the mind, let thoughts take flight,
As riddles bloom in evening light.

Beneath the Surface of Still Waters

Reflections shimmer, smooth and clear,
Holding stories whispered near.
Ripples dance, a fleeting touch,
What hides beneath is called by much.

Silent depths hold untold grace,
Where shadows linger, time's embrace.
The world above seems far away,
In mystery's hold, I wish to stay.

Fish dart through the light and gloom,
With hidden secrets in their loom.
Every splash tells tales concealed,\nNature's wonders softly revealed.

Stillness reigns, a breath in time,
Where thoughts can drift and hearts can climb.
In the depths, life sways and swirls,
Beneath the surface, magic unfurls.

Lurking in the Corners of Curiosity

Shadows move where questions dwell,
In quiet nooks where stories tell.
Curiosity's flame ignites,
Awakening hidden delights.

The corners hold a whispering breeze,
Secrets rustling through the trees.
In every glance, a new surprise,
Each turn reveals an endless prize.

With open hearts, we dare to seek,
The mysteries woven, mild and meek.
Every glance, a chance to find,
The stories left by the unkind.

Lurking thoughts in spaces bright,
Urgent yearnings for the light.
In curiosity, life expands,
Bridging gaps with gentle hands.

The Map of Unseen Paths

Beneath the stars, a map unfolds,
With trails of silver, dreams retold.
Each step leads to a world anew,
With possibilities waiting for you.

Winding roads through fields of lore,
Ancient signs and whispered more.
Footprints linger in morning dew,
Inviting wanderers, brave and true.

Waves of grass, a silent guide,
As seekers brave the ocean's tide.
In every turn, the heart will know,
The secrets only journeys show.

Adventure beckons, softly calls,
In the silence, the spirit sprawls.
Let courage lead, let fear depart,
To find the map that leads the heart.

Shadowed Pathways

Beneath the trees where whispers dwell,
The shadows dance with secrets to tell.
Footsteps lost in the twilight's embrace,
Tracing the lines of a mysterious place.

A lantern glows with a flickering light,
Guiding the wanderer through the night.
Every turn holds a tale untold,
A journey of courage, a heart bold.

Leaves rustle softly, the wind's soft sigh,
Murmurs of dreams that drift and fly.
In this quiet, dark, winding way,
The path reveals what words cannot say.

So step with grace, let your spirit roam,
In shadowed pathways, find your home.
With each heartbeat, let the magic grow,
A world of wonder waits for you to know.

Beyond the Veil

In the stillness, a hush falls near,
A veil of mist where spirits adhere.
Beyond the dawn, in realms unseen,
The fabric of life, intricate and keen.

There lies a world, both vast and deep,
Where the lost awaken from ancient sleep.
Shadows glide on air of gold,
In whispers of stories long grown bold.

Glimmers of hope, flickers of grace,
In every moment, a sacred space.
Transformations dance like wildfire's glow,
Beyond the veil, mysteries flow.

So tread with care through realms unknown,
Embrace the magic that feels like home.
In dreams unfurling, let your heart sail,
For the ephemeral beckons, beyond the veil.

Echoes of the Unexplored

In the silence, echoes softly call,
Resonating deep, a siren's thrall.
Footprints scattered on uncharted ground,
Where whispers of ancient truths abound.

The landscape hums with stories old,
Hidden treasures of dreams untold.
Every shadow sings in twilight's glow,
Secrets waiting for the brave to know.

Winding rivers and mountains high,
Beneath the vast and open sky.
In the pulse of nature's heartbeat lies,
A tapestry woven with heartfelt sighs.

So venture forth, embrace the thrill,
Of each new day, let curiosity fill.
In the echoes of what yet to find,
The unmasked wonders of the mind.

Treasures of the Abyss

Diving deep through the ocean's veil,
Hushed whispers carried by a gentle gale.
The depths conceal their shimmering might,
In shadows where darkness meets the light.

Coral gardens and sunken dreams,
Beneath the surface, the mystery gleams.
Every treasure holds a tale of old,
In the stillness, secrets unfold.

In the heart's abyss, a longing stirs,
For the depths of truth that quietly whirs.
The ocean's song, a melodic plea,
Calling the brave to dive and see.

So plunge with courage, let go of fear,
For treasures waiting are always near.
In the depths where the unknown sways,
Lie the wonders of the ocean's ways.

On the Edge of Inquisition

Questions linger in the air,
Whispers dance through the despair.
Seeking truths both near and far,
Underneath the watchful star.

The mind ignites with sparks of doubt,
What's hidden deep begins to shout.
We chase the shadows, hunt the light,
In quest of reason through the night.

Each answer leads to further streams,
A web of thoughts and tangled dreams.
With every step, we tread the line,
The edge of knowing, so divine.

And though the path may twist and turn,
Our hearts are filled with quiet yearn.
For in each question lies the key,
To unlock all we wish to see.

Unseen Echoes of Tomorrow

In whispered winds, the future calls,
With every shift, a shadow falls.
Promises of what's yet to come,
Resonate like distant drums.

The world spins on, both fast and slow,
With unseen tides that ebb and flow.
In every breath, a tale unfolds,
Of dreams untold and hopes behold.

Each moment gathers at the seam,
Where history meets the waking dream.
In echoes soft, we find our way,
Towards the dawn of a new day.

Let us dance with time's embrace,
And hold our future, face to face.
For in the silent space we toil,
Unseen seeds of change will boil.

The Pulse of the Unlikelihood

In every heart, a rhythm beats,
Defying odds, the spirit meets.
Against the flow, it dares to rise,
A spark of hope beneath the skies.

Chance and fate entwined in dance,
The unexpected takes its stance.
Amongst the chaos, dreams ignite,
And brush the shadows with their light.

From silent whispers, courage springs,
A life transformed, the joy it brings.
In unlikelihood, we find our soul,
Each leap of faith makes the heart whole.

So let us chase the bold unknown,
With every step, we're not alone.
For in the pulse of life's delight,
Unlikely paths can lead to light.

Where Silence Unleashes Curiosity

In quietude, the mind takes flight,
A realm of wonders, pure and bright.
Where thoughts unfold without a sound,
In stillness, hidden truths are found.

The gentle hush invites a quest,
Beneath the surface, thoughts contest.
A spark ignites, a question stirs,
In silence, life's enchantment whirs.

With eager hearts, we dare to ask,
What secrets hide beneath the mask?
In pondered moments, magic grows,
As silence weaves its subtle prose.

So hold your breath, embrace the pause,
For in the still, we find the cause.
Where silence lives, curiosity thrives,
Awakening the spark of lives.

Labyrinths of Thought

In the maze of my mind, I wander,
Lost in corners, shadows grow fonder.
Each twist and turn a whispered sigh,
Echoes of dreams that drift and die.

Paths intertwine like tangled vines,
Searching for wisdom within the signs.
Silent whispers guide my way forth,
Yet all I find is a deeper dearth.

Moments flicker like fleeting flames,
Illusions of truth hide their names.
While echoes chase what's lost in the haze,
The labyrinth of thought holds its gaze.

Threads of ideas, frayed and worn,
Weave the fabric of what's forlorn.
Through the depths, a flicker of light,
In the labyrinth, I seek the night.

Masks of the Familiar

Behind the smiles, faces conceal,
Stories and secrets that souls reveal.
Each mask worn on a delicate face,
Hiding emotions in this crowded space.

In laughter's echo, sadness strays,
As familiarity cloaks the play.
A dance of hearts, so deftly spun,
Yet deep inside, we come undone.

Chameleon souls, shifting and bright,
Blending with shadows, avoiding the light.
If only we dared to show what's real,
To cast aside the masks we conceal.

In whispered truths and aching sighs,
Beneath the surface, the spirit cries.
Let us unveil what we hold tight,
In the warmth of the genuine light.

In Search of Lost Light

Once bright and warm, now ghostly pale,
Echoes of laughter begin to fail.
Through corridors where shadows creep,
I chase the glimmers, in silence, steep.

Flickering memories, like stars in the night,
Guide my weary heart to what feels right.
Fragments of joy amidst shadows cast,
Hope whispers softly, saying, 'Hold fast.'

With every step, the dawn appears,
Illuminating roads once fraught with fears.
In the garden of dreams, I seek the sun,
Discovering warmth where I once could run.

In the tapestry of what has been lost,
Beauty remains despite the cost.
A flickering flame, still in my sight,
Forever I wander, in search of lost light.

The Uncharted Mind

Through the depths of thought I shall tread,
Where paths unseen continually spread.
Each turn a question, swirling and bold,
In the uncharted, mysteries unfold.

Ideas merge in a vibrant stream,
Reality dances, a delicate dream.
Untamed whispers beckon me near,
In the silence, I embrace my fear.

With every heartbeat, the shadows play,
Mapping the realms where thoughts drift away.
A compass of wonder, guiding me through,
Charting the unknown, a quest to pursue.

In the landscape of musings confined,
Lies the true essence of the uncharted mind.
With each discovery, the world unwinds,
As I journey deeper, to learn what binds.

Glimmers of the Invisible

In shadows dance the silent dreams,
Flickers of light, threaded seams,
Whispers of hope in the dark night,
Glimmers that guide with gentle might.

The unseen paths stretch far and wide,
Alongside questions that we confide,
Every breath holds a secret too,
Revealing glimpses of what is true.

Through misty fogs, we tread so light,
Curious hearts seeking the bright,
Fragments of truth in each new dawn,
Exploring the depths of the unknown.

With eyes wide open, we chase the stars,
Boundless dreams and invisible scars,
In the quiet, the glimmers spark,
A dance of shadows, igniting the dark.

Journey into the Heart of Mystery

Steps taken on the winding road,
Each turn a tale waiting to be showed,
The labyrinth calls, with secrets to keep,
In the heart of mystery, we leap.

Veils of silence cloak hidden truths,
Guiding our souls, rekindling youth,
Every heartbeat feels the pull,
As we wade through wonders, beautiful.

The winds whisper softly at our ears,
Echoes of laughter, joy and fears,
A compass of feelings leads the way,
Through shadows of night into the day.

In the tapestry woven with fate,
Threads intertwine, we hesitate,
Yet onward we move, undeterred,
Journeying forth, as souls conferred.

Fathoms of Forgotten Whispers

In the depths where silence lies,
Fathoms wade through unseen sighs,
Gentle echoes of stories past,
Whispers lingering, seemed to last.

Underneath the surface calm,
Memories weave like a soothing balm,
Glimmering eyes of ancient lore,
Calling us gently to seek and explore.

Each murmur flows through the midnight air,
A language lost in the depths of care,
Delicate threads of time so frail,
In each forgotten whisper, we unveil.

So listen close to the echoes deep,
The tales of old that softly seep,
In fathoms found, we seek our place,
In the whispering tides of time and space.

The Horizon of Uncertainty

Across the dunes where shadows blend,
The horizon stretches, curves around the bend,
With colors spilling into the day,
Uncertainty dances, leading the way.

Each footstep echoes of what's unknown,
As we chase dreams that feel like home,
The sun dips low, painting skies anew,
In this space, we find our truth.

Clouds whisper secrets of distant lands,
Guiding our hearts with invisible hands,
Every moment holds both fear and grace,
In the horizon's embrace, we find our place.

Beyond the edge, where visions fade,
Lies the promise of journeys made,
With each dawn, we face our fate,
The horizon calls, we hesitate.

Whispered Legends of Old

In shadows deep, the tales arise,
Of heroes lost and whispered sighs.
Beneath the stars, their stories gleam,
In quiet nights, we dare to dream.

The echoes call from ages past,
A fleeting glimpse, a shadow cast.
Through ancient woods, the spirits roam,
In every heart, they find a home.

With every breath, the legends flow,
In whispered tones, their wisdom grow.
The flames of truth dance in the dark,
Igniting hope, a vital spark.

So gather 'round, and lend your ear,
For faintest whispers we might hear.
Each legend holds a seed of light,
A guiding star in endless night.

Flickering Flames of Inquiry

In quiet corners, questions rise,
Flickering flames beneath the skies.
Each thought a spark, a flame of gold,
Igniting minds with tales untold.

Curiosity fuels our sight,
Chasing shadows, seeking light.
What mysteries lie in the unknown?
With every step, our minds have grown.

Constructing bridges from quest to quest,
In seeking answers, we find rest.
Each flame of inquiry, bright and bold,
Living stories begin to unfold.

So let us wander, lose the fear,
In flickering flames, the truth draws near.
For in the dance of thought and time,
Discovery is the greatest rhyme.

Parsing the Fog of Time

Through misty veils, the past unfolds,
Stories buried, secrets told.
In gentle whispers, echoes find,
Clarity within the mind.

With every step, the fog will clear,
Revealing paths, drawing near.
Moments captured, like fleeting dreams,
In the haze, the heart redeems.

We sift the sands of ages gone,
With patience, as we carry on.
Each fragment pieced, a puzzle true,
The timeless dance of me and you.

So let us roam through layers vast,
Parsing what's present, future, past.
For in the fog, the truth aligns,
A tapestry throughout the times.

Discoveries in the Abyss

In darkness deep, the wonders lie,
Where silence sings and shadows sigh.
In each abyss, a hidden spark,
Awakening dreams from depths so stark.

With courage firm, we dive below,
Through winding paths, where currents flow.
The heart of darkness bears its gifts,
In quiet depths, the spirit lifts.

What treasures wait in ocean's keep?
Ancient secrets, buried deep.
From sunken ships to tales untread,
In every wave, adventures spread.

So plunge into the depths we seek,
For every whisper, every peak.
Discoveries in the abyss await,
Within the dark, the world creates.

In the Shadow of Whispers

In the night where shadows play,
Secrets linger, softly sway,
Voices murmur, low and sweet,
Hiding truths beneath our feet.

Moonlight glimmers, faint and clear,
Tales of longing, tales of fear,
Each whisper paints a tale so bright,
In the silence of the night.

Beneath the stars, we find our muse,
In whispered dreams, we dare to choose,
Eclipsed by doubt, yet still we chase,
The warm embrace of timeless grace.

In secret glades, where shadows thrive,
We gather hope, we feel alive,
But in the dark, the truth may bend,
A fragile bond that has no end.

The Dance of Hidden Truths

In the quiet, secrets swirl,
Beneath the surface, truths unfurl,
Step by step, we weave and sway,
In hidden realms where shadows play.

Each heartbeat echoes in the night,
While darkness veils the fading light,
In this dance, we lose our guise,
Finding solace in our lies.

With each turn, a story grows,
In veils of mist, the silence flows,
Through whispered breaths, the heart engages,
The hidden truths of endless pages.

As we twirl, they intertwine,
Secrets linger, yours and mine,
In this waltz where souls collide,
Revealing depths we cannot hide.

Echoes of the Unfathomed

In the depths of echoing dreams,
Mysterious depths and hidden streams,
Whispers linger, softly weave,
Promises held, yet hard to believe.

In shadows cast by twilight's glow,
Secrets tremble, rarely show,
Each echo calls from distant place,
Chasing shadows, we find our grace.

With every pulse, the memories play,
In unfathomed realms, we drift away,
Floating on a echoing tide,
A journey where our truths abide.

As we wander through quiet halls,
We hear the silence when it calls,
In echoes lost, we rise anew,
Seeking beauty in the blue.

Beyond the Veil of Perception

Beyond the veil where visions blend,
A world awakens, twists and bends,
Through layers deep, we seek to find,
The unseen threads that bind mankind.

Here colors bloom in silent flight,
Shadows dance with pure delight,
In hidden corners, truths ignite,
Guiding hearts through endless night.

With eyes half-closed, we learn to see,
The whispers of what's meant to be,
In dreams that fail to fade away,
The sacred sparks of night and day.

So let us journey on this quest,
To grasp the heart of nature's best,
In the depths of perception's weave,
We find the magic we believe.

Quest for the Elusive

In fields of dreams, I wander slow,
Where whispers dance and secrets flow.
A spark of hope, a fleeting sight,
I chase the shadows, lost in light.

The stars above, they guide my way,
Through fog and mist, I will not sway.
With every step, a heartbeat's race,
In search of truth, I find my place.

The winds carry tales from afar,
Each moment captured, like a star.
I dive into the depths of night,
To grasp the dreams, to hold them tight.

Though paths may twist and turn unknown,
My spirit's flame, it has been sown.
With every quest, I learn to trust,
In shadows lies the spark of lust.

The Abyss of Possibility

In silence deep, the echoes play,
Lost in the void, I drift away.
The realm of dreams, a shapeless sea,
Invites the heart to wander free.

A fragile thread of fate unfolds,
Stories yet untold, adorned in gold.
Each choice I make, a path ignites,
In shadows cast by distant lights.

With every breath, the pulse of chance,
A cosmic dance, an endless trance.
I dive into the depths obscure,
Where hope and fear, they intertwine, pure.

The whispered thoughts of what could be,
Awake my soul, they set it free.
Through endless night, I learn to see,
The vast expanse, my destiny.

Chasing the Furtive Light

Across the hills, the shadows creep,
A flicker shines, my heart will leap.
In twilight's grasp, I run, I chase,
The furtive light, a fleeting grace.

With every step, the earth will sigh,
As dreams take flight across the sky.
I wander trails where lost hopes lie,
And seek the spark that cannot die.

The path is lined with tales of old,
Adventures stitched in threads of gold.
I chase the dawn, with breathless might,
In constant pursuit of hidden light.

Though shadows loom, and doubt may grow,
The spark within will always glow.
In every heart, a beacon bright,
Together, we chase the furtive light.

Hidden Patterns in the Dark

In velvet night, a tapestry weaves,
Patterns hidden, like secrets it leaves.
The stars align in whispers shared,
Each flicker a truth, silently bared.

The cosmos hums a silent song,
As shadows dance where dreams belong.
In stillness found, the answers rise,
Through veils of night, in midnight skies.

I ponder softly the paths I tread,
Through tangled thoughts, where fears are fed.
But in the dark, the beauty glows,
In hidden patterns, wisdom flows.

With every breath, I learn to see,
The light found deep inside of me.
In the mystery of the night,
I find my strength, I find my light.

Tapestry of Forgotten Tales

In the quiet dusk, whispers weave,
Old secrets linger, quietly grieve.
Threads of memories, colors faint,
Woven together in a tapestry quaint.

Stories hidden in fabric's embrace,
A time-worn journey, a sacred space.
Faded echoes of laughter and tears,
Revealing the truth of bygone years.

In shadowed corners, the past resides,
Each stitch a moment, where time abides.
Dreams once cherished, now softly tread,
In the tapestry's heart, where all is said.

With every thread, a life is spun,
In the light of memories, we become one.
Through colors vibrant and tales obscure,
The tapestry whispers, forever pure.

Shadows of the Unspoken

In the depths of silence, shadows creep,
Secrets linger where the heartbeats weep.
Words unvoiced in the night's embrace,
Echoes of thoughts, a ghostly trace.

Fears take flight in the moon's soft glow,
Whispered confessions that none can know.
Inkling of truth in the stillness found,
Where silence reigns and doubts abound.

The weight of silence, it binds so tight,
Casting shadows that blur the light.
In every heartbeat, a story waits,
Tangled in dreams, locked behind gates.

Yet in the shadows, a spark ignites,
Unspoken words take on new heights.
Through darkened paths, a truth shall rise,
Emerging softly beneath the skies.

The Allure of Enigma

Wrapped in the mystery, drawn to the night,
Secrets glimmer, cloaked in delight.
A puzzle of whispers, soft and subtle,
In shadows we wander, hearts in a muddle.

The allure of questions, where answers flee,
In the dance of unknown, we long to be free.
Layers of riddles, each twist a tease,
In the depth of enigma, we're lost with ease.

Curiosity blooms like stars in the dark,
Illuminating paths, igniting a spark.
Each flicker a story, a chance to explore,
In the realm of enigma, we yearn for more.

Yet wisdom whispers, so softly, so near,
In the heart of the mystery, there's nothing to fear.
Embrace the unknown, let the journey unfold,
For in every enigma, new truths are told.

Constellations of Concealed Stories

In the velvety night, stars softly gleam,
Each twinkle a story, a forgotten dream.
Constellations hint at fables untold,
Mapping the universe in whispers of old.

Galaxies spin in a dance of light,
Drawing us close with their mystical sight.
Each star a beacon, a fragment of fate,
Carrying tales from the hands of the late.

Beneath the wide heavens, we search the skies,
Hoping to find what in darkness lies.
Hidden in silence, stories await,
In the constellations, we contemplate.

With each fallen star, a wish takes flight,
A quest for the truth in the blanket of night.
So gaze at the heavens, let your heart see,
The concealed stories that yearn to be free.

Twists in the Tapestry

Threads woven tight, colors collide,
Stories unfold, in whispers they bide.
Patterns emerge from shadows and light,
Each twist a secret, in fabric's delight.

A dance of fate, in loom's embrace,
Threads of joy meet threads of grace.
An intricate world, a vibrant weave,
In every knot, a tale we believe.

Life's tapestry grows, day by day,
With every turn, in a unique way.
Unseen hands guide the work we do,
In every thread, a part of you.

So, cherish the folds, the bends in the seam,
For in their design, lies the heart's dream.
In colors and patterns, the truth you find,
A living mosaic, forever entwined.

Embracing the Unknown

In twilight's glow, shadows dance,
A step beyond, we choose to glance.
The path ahead, a hazy sight,
Yet hearts ignite with hopeful light.

Curiosity blooms like flowers fair,
In the wild winds, we lay bare.
Each unknown turn, a beckoning call,
To venture forth, to rise or fall.

Fears are whispers, soft and weak,
Bravery grows in the words we speak.
Embrace the change, let hope unbind,
In the arms of night, our dreams aligned.

Together we wander, hand in hand,
Discovering worlds, so vast, so grand.
For in the dark, new stars will show,
Embracing the unknown, we learn to grow.

Beneath the Starlit Enigma

Under a sky where mysteries play,
Stars paint stories, light years away.
Veils of the cosmos, secrets unfold,
In the depth of night, wonders untold.

Whispers of stardust, dreams take flight,
In celestial realms, we chase the night.
A canvas vast, in darkness concealed,\nThe heartbeat of galaxies, gently revealed.

Echoes of laughter from distant stars,
Binding the universe, no earthly bars.
In cosmic embrace, we dance and sway,
Learning the language of shadows at play.

In the silence of space, we find our song,
Beneath the starlit enigma, we belong.
With every twinkle, a promise rings clear,
In the vastness of night, we're ever near.

Refracted Dreams in Twilight

As daylight wanes, colors blur,
In twilight's grasp, soft visions stir.
Dreams refracted through prismed skies,
A symphony of hopes that never dies.

Through the haze, shadows meld,
In the dance of dusk, our hearts compelled.
Each whispered wish, like shimmering dew,
In twilight's glow, feels fresh and new.

Moments linger in the fading light,
Painting our dreams, embracing the night.
With every breath, the world unwinds,
Refracted hopes, the heart defines.

So chase the glow where dreams take form,
In twilight's arms, we weather the storm.
Together we'll find, in colors that gleam,
The beauty of life, in every dream.

Unfurling the Canvas

Colors blend in quiet grace,
Brushstrokes dance in soft embrace.
A story waits beneath the hue,
Unfurling dreams in shades anew.

Whispers echo on the ground,
Each layer speaks without a sound.
The heart unfolds with every line,
A canvas bright, a life divine.

Here, hopes flicker and ignite,
In artistic flames, they take flight.
A masterpiece of tender care,
Each stroke a love song in the air.

With every color, life is spun,
In the gallery, we become one.
A journey vast as time can bend,
Unfurling stories, trends transcend.

The Allure of the Abyss

Beneath the waves, the secrets sigh,
Whispers soft, where shadows lie.
The moonlit pull, a call so deep,
In darkened waters, mysteries sleep.

Glistening depths, a haunting dance,
Where silence reigns, we take a chance.
Curiosity, it draws us near,
To the abyss, where dreams appear.

The pressure mounts with every gaze,
Yet still we dwell in the ocean's maze.
In liquid black, we find our way,
The allure of the night, a moonlit sway.

Awash with wonders yet to know,
In depths where no light dares to go.
We dive, we plunge, we chase the night,
Into the void, our spirits take flight.

Tales from the Shadows

In twilight's grip, the stories weave,
Darkened corners, a breath to leave.
Echoes linger where silence speaks,
In shadows cast, the secret seeks.

Figures dance in fleeting light,
Fragments of life now take their flight.
Whispers tell of love and woe,
In every dark, the dreams still glow.

Histories etched in the night's embrace,
Lurking tales in forgotten space.
Each shadow holds a memory dear,
A world concealed, yet ever near.

Eclipsed in dusk, they find their breath,
Stories born of life and death.
In shadows deep, we find a way,
To tell the tales the light won't say.

The Depths of Curiosity

Waves of wonder crash and swell,
In the heart of night, we yearn to dwell.
Questions bloom like flowers bright,
Seeking truth in shadows' light.

With every step, the path unfurls,
In the maze of thought, our mind twirls.
A quest to know, to understand,
The universe at our command.

Secrets whisper in the breeze,
Calling forth our restless pleas.
In every nook and cranny explored,
Curiosity's ship, forever soared.

To dive into the unknown sea,
A hunger, an endless decree.
In the depths of questions, we find the key,
Unlocking worlds of infinity.

Veils of Mystery

In shadows deep, the secrets lie,
Veils of mist that echo sighs.
Ancient tales in silence sleep,
Guarded dreams our hearts will keep.

Through the dark, a flicker glows,
Hints of truths that no one knows.
The night conceals, the dawn reveals,
A world alive with silent wheels.

Whispers drift on the evening breeze,
Softly weaving through the trees.
Each rustle speaks of things untold,
In twilight's arms, the secrets unfold.

Here in the stillness, take a breath,
For life awakens even in death.
Veils may shroud, but hope will rise,
In the heart where mystery lies.

Secrets Beneath the Surface

Beneath the calm, a tempest roars,
Hidden thoughts behind closed doors.
Ripples dance on the water's skin,
Where shadows play and stories begin.

Silent depths hold tales of yore,
Whispers echo from the ocean floor.
Each wave conceals a world apart,
Secrets wrapped in nature's art.

Under the moon, in tides that swell,
Lies the rhythm of a hidden spell.
The surface sparkles, but deeper lies,
A realm untouched by prying eyes.

In silence, truths will shimmer bright,
Drawing wanderers into the night.
What we see is but a show,
Beneath the surface, mysteries flow.

Whispers of the Unseen

In the quiet corners where shadows dwell,
Soft whispers weave their secret spell.
Ghostly echoes of the past,
Stories linger, though time won't last.

Invisible threads tie hearts and minds,
Through the silence, connection finds.
Each sigh a story, each breath a song,
In the fabric where we all belong.

Glimmers of light through the haze appear,
Messages carried from those held dear.
As we journey through the night,
Unseen hands guide us to the light.

Let the whispers fill the air,
With tales of love and gentle care.
For in the unseen, we find our way,
Through the darkness to the light of day.

The Hidden Threads

In the tapestry of life we weave,
Hidden threads that we can't perceive.
Connections made by fate's own hand,
Binding souls in a silent strand.

Every moment, a stitch in time,
Lost in the rhythm, a secret rhyme.
We are woven with dreams and fears,
Threads of laughter, woven tears.

Through the fabric, patterns unfold,
Stories of courage, tales retold.
Each thread a path, a chance embrace,
In the loom of life, we find our place.

As we look closely, we may discern,
The hidden threads from which we learn.
In unity, we find our blend,
Woven together, until the end.

Lattice of Unsung Stories

In quiet corners, tales reside,
Whispers linger where shadows hide.
Each thread woven, a life unseen,
Moments lost, between the green.

The laughter echoes, the tears cascade,
History crafted, memories made.
Silent screams in the night take flight,
Unsung heroes fade out of sight.

A tapestry rich, of joy and pain,
Each story whispers in the rain.
Yet in the silence, truths unfold,
Threads of life in colors bold.

Within these lines, new paths align,
A lattice formed by fate's design.
Each heartbeat counts, a pulse so strong,
In unsung stories, we all belong.

Threads of Fate in Shadows

In the twilight where secrets weave,
Fate threads shadows, seldom seen.
Each step a dance on paths unknown,
Unraveled dreams in twilight's throne.

Whispers of time in the gentle breeze,
Stitching moments with silent ease.
Every choice echoes in the dark,
A flickering flame, a guiding spark.

Into the depths where fear resides,
Beneath the masks that time abides.
We journey forth through hazy nights,
Seeking truth in the morning lights.

With threads of fate, we weave our song,
In shadowed corners, we all belong.
Tales untold in the quiet sigh,
Threads unite as the stars reply.

The Unseen Archives of Time

In dusty tomes, the stories sleep,
Forgotten echoes, memories deep.
Pages whisper of lives once bright,
In unseen archives, out of sight.

Chapters lost in the haze of years,
Chronicles penned with blood and tears.
The ticking clock marks each refrain,
Every heartbeat held in time's chain.

As moments flicker like candlelight,
Fragments gather in the quiet night.
The past unfolds in a silent breath,
Unseen archives, a dance with death.

We search for meaning in faded lines,
Each story stitched where history twines.
In the heart of time, we find our way,
In the unseen realms where shadows sway.

Cracks in the Facade of Reality

In the mirror, a glimpse remains,
Cracks appear, like whispered stains.
Reality bends, a fragile thread,
What's left unsaid, what's left for dead.

Behind the curtain, truths expose,
Fissures form where darkness grows.
Every lie, a jagged line,
In fractured worlds, we search for signs.

The weight of dreams on weary backs,
In the twilight, we find our tracks.
With every heartbeat, the tension swells,
In cracks of facade, the silence yells.

We grasp at shadows drifting past,
Hoping for solace, hoping to last.
Yet in the fractures, we find our own,
In cracks and crevices, seeds are sown.

Milton Keynes UK
Ingram Content Group UK Ltd.
UKHW021129021124
0571UK00005B/81

9 789916 902905